A Real Nice Clambake evokes the sights and sounds of
an old-fashioned New England clambake. The text,
by Oscar Hammerstein II, is written in a dialect common
to the region a century ago.

First Edition

Library of Congress Cataloging-in-Publication Data

Hammerstein, Oscar, 1865 – 1960.
    A real nice clambake / lyrics by Oscar Hammerstein II ; music by
Richard Rodgers ; illustrations by Nadine Bernard Westcott. —1st ed.
        p.   cm.
    Lyrics taken from Rodgers and Hammerstein's musical *Carousel*.
    Summary: Family and friends gather on a New England beach to savor
the wonderful foods at a clambake.
    ISBN 0-316-75422-6
    1. Songs — United States — Texts. [Picnicking — Songs and music.
2. Food — Songs and music. 3. Beaches — Songs and music. 4. New
England — Songs and music. 5. Songs.] I. Rodgers, Richard, 1902 –.
II. Westcott, Nadine Bernard, ill. III. Title.
PZ8.3.H1865Re   1992
[E]—dc20   91-21913

Joy Street Books are published by Little, Brown and Company (Inc.)

10 9 8 7 6 5 4 3 2 1

NIL

Published simultaneously in Canada
by Little, Brown & Company (Canada) Limited

Printed in Italy

A Real Nice Clambake

Lyrics by Oscar Hammerstein II
Music by Richard Rodgers
Illustrations by Nadine Bernard Westcott

JOY STREET BOOKS

Little, Brown and Company
Boston Toronto London

This was a real nice clambake,

We're mighty glad we came.

The vittles we et were good, you bet!

The company was the same.

Our hearts are warm, our bellies are full,

And we are feelin' prime.

This was a real nice clambake,

And we all had a real good time.

First come codfish chowder,
Cooked in iron kettles,

Onions floatin' on the top,
Curlin' up in petals.

Throwed in ribbons of salted pork
(An old New England trick)

And lapped it all up with a clamshell,
Tied on to a bayberry stick.

Oh-h-h —
This was a real nice clambake,
We're mighty glad we came.
The vittles we et
Were good, you bet!
The company was the same.

Our hearts are warm,
Our bellies are full,
And we are feelin' prime.
This was a real nice clambake,
And we all had a real good time.

Remember when we raked
Them red-hot lobsters
Out of the driftwood fire?

They sizzled and crackled
And sputtered a song,
Fitten fer an angels' choir.
    Fitten fer an angels',
    Fitten fer an angels',
    Fitten fer an angels' choir!

We slit 'em down the back
And peppered 'em good,
And doused 'em in melted butter —

Then we tore away the claws
And cracked 'em with our teeth
'Cause we weren't in the mood to putter! . . .

Fitten fer an angels',
Fitten fer an angels',
Fitten fer an angels' choir!

Then at last come the clams,
Steamed under rockweed
An' poppin' from their shells —
Jest how many of 'em
Galloped down our gullets
We couldn't say oursel's!

Oh-h-h —
This was a real nice clambake,
We're mighty glad we came.
The vittles we et
Were good, you bet!
The company was the same.

Our hearts are warm,
Our bellies are full,
And we are feelin' prime.
This was a real nice clambake,
And we all had a real good time.

We said it afore —
And we'll say it agen —
We all had a real good time!

A Real Nice Clambake